Survival Guide:
20 Useful Tips How To Live Without Electricity And Survive A Blackout

All photos used in this book, including the cover photo were made available under a Attribution-NonCommercial-ShareAlike 2.0 Generic and sourced from Flickr

Copyright 2016 by the publisher - All rights reserved.

This document is geared towards providing exact and reliable information in regards to the topic and issue covered. The publication is sold with the idea that the publisher is not required to render accounting, officially permitted, or otherwise, qualified services. If advice is necessary, legal or professional, a practiced individual in the profession should be ordered.

- From a Declaration of Principles which was accepted and approved equally by a Committee of the American Bar Association and a Committee of Publishers and Associations.

In no way is it legal to reproduce, duplicate, or transmit any part of this document in either electronic means or in printed format. Recording of this publication is strictly prohibited and any storage of this document is not allowed unless with written permission from the publisher. All rights reserved.

The information provided herein is stated to be truthful and consistent, in that any liability, in terms of inattention or otherwise, by any usage or abuse of any policies, processes, or directions contained within is the solitary and utter responsibility of the recipient reader. Under no circumstances will any legal responsibility or blame be held against the publisher for any reparation, damages, or monetary loss due to the information herein, either directly or indirectly.

Respective authors own all copyrights not held by the publisher.

The information herein is offered for informational purposes solely, and is universal as so. The presentation of the information is without contract or any type of guarantee assurance.

The trademarks that are used are without any consent, and the publication of the trademark is without permission or backing by the trademark owner. All trademarks and brands within this book are for clarifying purposes only and are the owned by the owners themselves, not affiliated with this document.

Table of Contents

★ ★ ★ ★ ★ ★ ★ ★ ★ ★ ★ ★ ★ ★ ★ ★

Introduction: Getting Rid of the Grid 6

Chapter 1: Living off the Sun 7

    Tip Number 1: Learn the Nuts and Bolts of a Solar Panel 7

    Tip Number 2: Use Deep Cycle Batteries 8

    Tip Number 3: Understand How Solar Inverters Work 9

    Tip Number 4: Hybridize with Solar Powered Generators 10

    Tip Number 5: Try Second Hand Solar Cells 11

    Tip Number 6: Building your Very Own Solar Panel System 12

    Tip Number 7: Know Proper Wire Installation Technique 13

Chapter 2: Heat and Fuel when the Power Goes Out 14

    Tip Number 8: Emergency Fuel Additives 14

    Tip Number 9: Utilize Fuel Cells 15

    Tip Number 10: Clean Burning Wood Stove 16

    Tip Number 11: Create DIY Candle Crayons 16

Chapter 3: Finding Water in the Dark 18

    Tip Number 12: Turn Your Bathtub into a Water Storage Unit 18

    Tip Number 13: Save water in your Sinks 19

    Tip Number 14: Making Use of Water Heaters 20

    Tip Number 15: Capturing the Water in Your Household Pipes 21

    Tip Number 16: Taking Water from your Toilet Tank 21

    Tip Number 17: Don't Blame it on the Rain! Use a Rain Barrel! 22

Chapter 4: Survival Communication During a Blackout 23

    Tip Number 18: C.B. Radio 23

    Tip Number 19: Hand Cranked Radio 24

    Tip Number 20: The Landline Phone 25

Conclusion: The Meaning of Survival 26

FREE Bonus Reminder 28

Introduction: Getting Rid of the Grid

Human beings have only been living with electricity for a little over 200 years, yet we are all quite dependant on that magical energy that come up through our power outlet. But have you ever been surprised by a blackout? Maybe you were minding your own business one evening, updating your Face Book page, and periodically watching a football game on the TV, when suddenly your house was thrown into complete darkness. Then perhaps you stumbled through the room attempting to see with the dying light of a cell phone you should have charged, in your attempt to figure out what's going on.

You then get the idea to place a phone call before your cell phone's battery dies, but once you do, you are in for yet another surprise. Because as soon as you attempt to dial out, the call drops and you realize that you currently have no service. You now have to come to grips with the fact that the whole entire grid that you relied upon for both power and communication has completely collapsed. What can you do? We are now so used to our constant connection to a centralized network; we wouldn't know what to do if we were suddenly unplugged from it.

In order to survive a blackout we will have to retrain our brain to not necessarily rely on massive corporations such as AT & T in order to communicate, or General Electric in order to have electricity, in the world of the failing grid we will need to move away from the massive bureaucracies that have had us locked in for so many years and learn to strike it out on our own. It may not be easy, but you have to make the first step towards elf sufficiency and after way too many years of dependence, tell yourself once and for all, that you will get rid of the grid!

Chapter 1: Living off the Sun

The sunlight that shines over us produces enough energy to power the entire planet for the next 500,000 years in just one second of sunlight hitting the Earth's surface! I didn't mean to make you choke on your coffee with such a mind boggling statement, but it is absolutely true! The only reason we are not all capitalizing on this little known fact is due to the inability of current technology to efficiently collect the huge amount of energy that the sun produces.

The best solar panels are typically only able to absorb about 20% of the sunlight that strikes their surface, but even though this is just a small fraction of what could be potentially harvested, that 20% can still achieve quite a bit when it come to independence from the grid. So if you would like to learn more about how solar power can gain you independence from electricity, keep reading!

<u>Tip Number 1: Learn the Nuts and Bolts of a Solar Panel</u>

The term "Solar Panel" is sort of a loaded word, because even though we refer to the whole system as a solar panel—as I will also do in this book—the panel involved in a so lar powered energy system is not the device that collects sunlight, the panel is simply the protective case that surrounds the sun reflective material called "solar cells". It is these solar cells that actually absorb energy from the sun, not the paneling itself.

The solar cells are made up of silicon which can break down light energy and hitting their surface. The silicon of the cell is made up of special atoms which react to the light they receive and are then able to transfer the energy they store into a direct power source. The average solar panel system should give you enough energy to keep your home up and running for a long time to come. So much so in fact, many have even been able to have enough left over power that they sold it right back to the electric companies. Talk about sticking it to the grid!

Tip Number 2: Use Deep Cycle Batteries

Deep Cycle Batteries are the units usually used to store all of the power transferred out of solar panel systems. These batteries can store this solar energy until they can be rerouted and sent to power up our energy hungry technology. Some have been under the false impression that they can simply hook up a car battery to their solar panels, but this is a bad idea. Car batteries were not meant to store large amounts of energy. Just think about it, what keeps your car battery running after prolonged use? Your car's alternator of course!

As anyone who has ever had a bad alternator in their car can attest, without that technological component constantly charging up their battery during use, their car's battery will soon be as dead as a doornail. Car battery's are typically low storage units and only have enough energy in their dormant state to start your car; it is your car's alternator that does the rest. So having that said, you can only imagine what happens when you rip a car battery out of a vehicle and attempt to use it as a storage battery, it simply doesn't work. Standard deep-cycle batteries however, are able to discharge nearly 80% of the energy they store without the battery going dead.

Tip Number 3: Understand How Solar Inverters Work

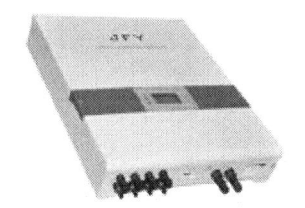

Power can not be gleaned from your deep cycle batteries until you run it through a Solar Inverter. The energy in your battery is in a state of DC (direct current) it is after running it through an inverter that it transforms into AC (alternating current) which can be utilized for electricity in your home. For each 12 volts of DC power held in a battery, about 120 volts of AC power can be generated.

And this is incidentally enough, another good reason to use a deep cycle battery rather than a car battery, because deep cycle batteries are designed to plug into specially made inverters, whereas a car battery is not. Most inverters plug directly into deep cycle batteries through a connector that look similar to the kind of plug you would stick in your car's cigarette lighter. This fixture from the inverter just plugs right into the deep cycle battery. The inverter once plugged in, can then be flipped over to reveal the 120 volt socket on the other side through which the Alternating Current it produces can be accessed.

Tip Number 4: Hybridize with Solar Powered Generators

As good as solar power is, it can be even more effective when you combine it with a good generator. Generators can be a great boost during the winter or during times of just heavy cloud cover when the sun's light is not able to penetrate down to your solar panels effectively. No matter what the cause however, if you have a trusty generator on hand, you can easily supplement the shortage.

The generator can be used to make sure your deep cycle batteries stay charged, just try not to over do it, because if you are not careful too much power from a generator can ruin your battery. Always use monitoring equipment to keep careful watch of the percentage of power in your batteries. As soon as your battery hits around 90% it's time to stop charging it. So just keep that in mind, and with an optimally running solar power system, you can quite literally save your generators for a rainy day!

Tip Number 5: Try Second Hand Solar Cells

I admit it obtaining second hand solar cells probably doesn't sound any more attractive than receiving used shoes from the Salvation Army, but in the case of solar power, gently used solar material is quite a good thing! By getting second hand, or even slightly damaged solar cells you could save a fortune, and the quality is usually not at all diminished in the process. You see, just because a solar panel is "used" or "blemished" doesn't mean they are ineffective, all it really means is that they have been taken out of their original packaging or maybe have been just slightly damaged—usually in the form of a chipped edge or slight dent.

These surface defects will not affect the solar cells ability to absorb sunlight however, making them still quite valuable for their main purpose; solar energy. Second hand solar cells are readily available on EBay, Amazon, and several other internet platforms. There are also whole forums that have been created allowing users sell or even trade their second hand solar cells to those who need them. This way you can get yourself some quality solar cells for a quality price.

Tip Number 6: Building your Very Own Solar Panel System

The first step of building your own Solar Panel System is to construct the solar panel itself. As mentioned earlier in this book, it is the solar panel that comprises the housing that the actual solar device sits in. Most solar panels consist of a flat rectangle. The solar cells are placed directly on this flat surface. In my experience I have found that good old fashioned peg board works extremely well for your panel's base. The grid-like design of the classic peg board is the perfect template for placing solar cells, because all you have to do is follow the squares already etched into the grid.

Simply cut your peg board to size and then use wood working glue to put your solar cells in place. Now just set this assembly to the side and allow it to dry for a few hours. While the solar cells are drying onto your peg board you can then work to construct a wooden housing for your pegboard. The easiest thing to do is to just take a few 2/4 pieces of wood which can be obtained from any home improvement store and lay them out horizontally on top of each other, now nail your pegboard onto these pieces of lumber and your main solar panel housing is complete.

Tip Number 7: Know Proper Wire Installation Technique

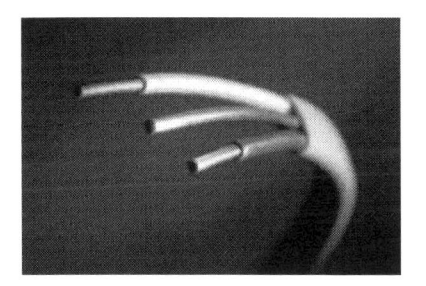

After creating your solar panel housing the next thing you need to arrange is the installation of your solar panel's wiring. It's not as hard s you might think. Just take a standard hand drill and bore a hole through the back of your peg board. It doesn't really matter that much where, just try to keep the hole close to the edges of the panel. Now you can run a wire through this hole straight to your solar cells. Next, place a polarized two pin plug at the end of your wire and plug it into your deep cycle battery. Finally attach a blocking diode to the other end and your homemade solar panel is ready for business.

Chapter 2: Heat and Fuel when the Power Goes Out

If you are living in North America in the middle of December and your power suddenly kicks off, it won't be long before you start feeling the full force of winter right within the walls of your home. Finding enough heat to be able to stay adequately warm is of tremendous important during a blackout that may disable more electric based heating apparatus. And along with heat sources for warmth, you will undoubtedly need a source for fuel. You will need fuel for vehicles and fuel for generators, read further to find out how you can manage to achieve both.

Tip Number 8: Emergency Fuel Additives

Isn't just your luck that Armageddon would hit right when your gas tank is on empty? Right when the Zombies are on your trail you see nothing but E! But don't worry, because if you read this book, you will be prepped with a ready made solution to bug out quick even on a fuel depleted vehicle. There are many great additives that can enhance your fuel but one of the best is a synthetic blend called "Magic Fuel". Even when your car is on empty, if you pour some "Magic Fuel" in the tank it's special chemicals will merge with the last drops of your fuel in your car and stretch them out enough to get to a gas station (if available) or at least to get yourself far away from any potential danger in an emergency.

Tip Number 9: Utilize Fuel Cells

Many are familiar with gaining power through solar cells but what about gaining a similar energy reaction through the use of fuel cells? Fuel cells are electrochemical devices that convert fuel directly into usable electricity and warmth from a chemical reaction between oxygen and hydrogen. Fuel cells were first invented in the 1800's but they weren't widely utilized until the Space Age when the chemical reactions of these cells were harnessed during the Apollo missions for safe, clean fuel.

Fuel cells can turn a simple chemical reaction into direct energy. These cells separate oxygen from hydrogen into an energizing catalyst. With a fuel cell system in the home you can produce moderate heating and electricity with very little waste. Fuel cells work by pumping fuel from a tank to a fuel processor, through a fuel cell stack, then on to a battery, to an inverter and then directly to home and devices as electricity and heat.

Tip Number 10: Clean Burning Wood Stove

This blackout DIY is a bit old school but it is highly efficient. The classic wood burning stove can easily heat a large section of your home. Invented by Benjamin Franklin there is nothing more quintessentially American than this wood burning dynamo. Before the wood stove people had to sit by the fireplace to stay warm, but this efficient wood burning box can be easily moved from room to room.

Tip Number 11: Create DIY Candle Crayons

Yes, crayons are good for more than coloring books. Because the lights go out and you are in a true emergency you can convert these wax based coloring utensils into the perfect fuel for an emergency set of candles. All you have to do is break off their ends—you don't even have to take the paper wrapping off—just light the broken tip and the paper wrap will serve as a makeshift wick. These candles can light up your house for next to nothing at all! If you have a box of 2 dollar crayola lying around feel free to use them to light up the house when the power goes out!

Chapter 3: Finding Water in the Dark

If the power suddenly cuts out on you and you are not able to make a trip to a local convenience store for a pack of Ice Mountain bottled water, you may need to take some matters into your own hands in order to have a viable water supply. When electricity and basic utilities go out due to storms or grid failures, your water supply is vulnerable. Tap water may become contaminated from flooding and other dangerous factors borne from the disturbance. In this chapter we will highlight some fo the best ways to secure and find your water supply, even in the dark.

Tip Number 12: Turn Your Bathtub into a Water Storage Unit

If you have a bit of forewarning that a bad storm or a power outage is going to strike your community then you can take some proactive action and fill your bathtub up with as much water as you can. It may not be too appealing to drink water stored in a place where you bathe, but if you run out of water at some point during the outage this bathtub contained H2O may very well save your life. If you have time, you can try to clean your tub so that it is a bit more palatable for water storage, but it really isn't necessary. Why isn't it necessary?

Because you will ultimately have to filter and boil the water anyway before you attempt to drink it. So cleaning the tub is mostly just a time wasting enterprise when your energy may very well be needed elsewhere during the crisis. And besides this, in all actuality attempts to clean the tub could in fact make matters worse, since the chemical that you use for tub cleaner will end up in the water that you are storing! Dirt and grime is one thing, but certain cleaning agents can be deadly! So be very careful about what you put on the surface of your tub before you consider storing water in inside of it.

Tip Number 13: Save water in your Sinks

Just like saving water in your bathtub, you can also save quite a bit of this liquid resource in your kitchen and bathroom sinks! Just open your taps and let each sink accumulate water until it is completely full. This standing water in your sinks can then later be moved to an easier to manage plastic or glass container. One of the easiest ways to collect this H2O is to stick a regular plastic bottle (like a used water bottle no less) down in the sink and let it naturally suction up as much water as the bottle can hold. Once your water is in your bottle just don't forget to sterilize it either by means of a filter, boiling or through chlorine tablets.

Tip Number 14: Making Use of Water Heaters

Most people don't realize this, but the home has an internally built water supply at hand at all times; the water heater! Basically a large cylindrical H2O storage depot, the water heater holds several gallons of water that are there just for the taking. This water was being used with the initial purpose of facilitating heat, so of course, extreme caution must be used in accessing it, and this means being sure that the water is completely cooled off.

And even though your power may already be out, to be sure, go ahead and move all the switches on your power breaker to the "off" position before you attempt to retrieve any water. Once you have followed these precautions you can then simply go underneath your water heater, grab hold of the lever and fill up a sturdy plastic container with the water that begins to flow out. Let this water sit for a moment or two, letting any dust and sediments fall to the bottom. And of course, you will want to filter or boil this water just to be sure it if safe to drink.

Tip Number 15: Capturing the Water in Your Household Pipes

Your household pipes have a lot of water trapped inside them at any given time. If the power suddenly goes out, the first thing that you should do is shut off the main line of water to your home so you can collect it. The water trapped inside your pipes should be free from contamination, so once the water is shut off and the H2O trapped, you can then easily take it out. In order to access this water, simply turn on your top (with the water line off) and it will come out just like it did in the past. It may be a bit slow at first though, coming out of the faucet as a trickle, but it should increase in volume enough to get a glass of water or fill up one of your containers.

Tip Number 16: Taking Water from your Toilet Tank

This one, no doubt sounds like one of the most disgusting things you have ever heard of, but when the spit hits the fan, and your house goes dark, you could find a source of water in the tank of your toilet. To use it, you must have your water line turned off, make sure that you don't let anyone in your home flush the toilet. To collect this water you might also want to wear some gloves, while the tank water is not as hazardous as toilet bowl water, it still no doubt has some bacteria floating in it, so while you are collecting it make sure to avoiding contact with your skin. Once the water is collected it can easily be sanitized through boiling it or using potent chlorine treatment.

Tip Number 17: Don't Blame it on the Rain! Use a Rain Barrel!

If it is pouring down rain, don't blame your luck that you were caught in a storm, instead you should take advantage of it! If your caught in a black out in the midst of a storm you can at least work to collect that very much drinkable rain water. The best way to use a rain barrel is to strategically place it underneath your gutter so that all of the rain hitting your roof can pull down into it. This rain will soon be running down into your barrel in torrents. One the barrel is full just be sure to boil the water, since your roof no doubt has some unpleasant contaminants that were probably picked up in the runoff.

Chapter 4: Survival Communication During a Blackout

For most of us, the scariest thing about a blackout would be not having any means of communication to the outside world. We can light a few candles and have the solace of being able to see in the dark, but if we become so isolated that we are unable to contact our friends and family we would start feeling pretty desperate for a means of communication pretty quick.

And since most of us rely on cell phones, a power outage could put the pressure on us pretty quick. Even a fully charged cell phone would be nearly exhausted in nearly a day, and even if the battery is charged, a massive blackout will more often than not, shut down enough cell phone towers to make our smart phones—well—not very smart at all! So having that said, in this chapter let's take a look at some of the best and most effective mean of survival communication during a blackout.

Tip Number 18: C.B. Radio

Yes, the communication bread and butter of the trucker could be your means of contacting the outside world during a blackout. If you have one installed in your car, an assuming that the battery of your vehicle isn't dead, you could easily hop on the old C.B. and let the rest of the world know that you are out there! And since C.B. is still the preferred method of choice for fire fighters, police, and paramedics all over the world, you will have access to the most direct link to emergency services. CB radio is a shortwave broadcast disseminated over multiple channels. When speaking through a CB channel, the broadcast works in a back and forth dialogue in which each speaker waits for the other speaker to finish their broadcast before responding.

Tip Number 19: Hand Cranked Radio

Amazingly, this radio does not need to be plugged in and it works even though batteries *are not* included! All you have to do I rapidly turn the crank on the side of the device and it will power up from the sheer force of the kinetic energy your hand creates from cranking the lever. Modern hand crank radios often also come with the highly beneficial addition of USB ports that can be used to charge up your cell phone's and tablets through the sheer force of your cranking hand! This is hand power at its finest! Your arm might get a work out but at least you can stay informed with this communication device!

Tip Number 20: The Landline Phone

You never thought that old antiquated landline phone would become a vital source of communication, but if the power goes out, the cell phone can't be charged, this ancestor of the mobile will be in the forefront once again as a reliable means of communication. Even if your cell phone is charged, and the cell towers are still running, in true emergencies, mobile phones have been proven to be completely unreliable since emergency situations cause everyone in your area to call at the same time and completely jam up the network!

But ah! The reliable old landline does not depend on such things! As long as your telephone poles aren't knocked down you should still be able to get through on a landline. And of course, the landline will not need to be charged since it is operating directly through an outside line. These are some of the best means of communication during a blackout!

Conclusion: The Meaning of Survival

A couple of summer's ago I had the privilege of making a trip to Ethiopia. This East African nation is one of the oldest, uninterrupted civilization's on the planet, with the notoriety of being the only African country on the continent to have never been conquered by a foreign power. Indeed, Ethiopian seems to carry a great legacy of innovative survival; a veritable paradise for the prepper survivalist!

But what impressed me the most during my sojourn in this legendary country was the way in which its citizens bore the brunt of their bloated bureaucracies' failing grid based power system. During my whole months in the country blackouts were epidemic. In fact, they were routine. Almost without a hitch, every three days, the capitol of Ethiopia, Addis Ababa, would be left without power, with the entire city in the dark. As a writer who was rather dependant on a fully charged lap top and at least the faint Wi-Fi of the local internet café's, I was at a loss.

But then I made a discovery. One day during the latest power outage I ran into a street vendor selling bottled water, feeling thirsty in the squelching heat I asked the gentlemen for a bottle of water. As I handed him his five Ethiopian Burr (Ethiopian money), I then just happened to notice a complete solar panel leaning up against his stall. I was quick to ask him where he got it from, and after a jumbled explanation of the winding streets of downtown Addis that I was still getting used to, I eventually found myself at one of the main luxury hotels in the region.

I was incredulous to say the least, at the thought of someone hawking solar panels in this swanky place. But when I walked into the lobby I looked to my left and saw a door cracked slightly open, and on the door just below the faded English words "Broom Closet" was a cheesy self-made flyer that read in big letters, "Solar Panels Here!" I stepped in and too my amazement in this tiny bit of closet space, this skinny old man was sitting on a stool with piles of solar panels at his feet!

As soon as the man saw me his face spread into a wide grin of pure joy as he motioned toward the solar panel's exclaiming, "Sir!! Sir!! Are you without electricity?! Come!! Come!! Survive the blackout! Come!!" It was in this literal hole in the wall that I learned the true meaning of ingenuity and survival!

FREE Bonus Reminder

If you have not grabbed it yet, please go ahead and download your special bonus E book *"Chakras for Beginners. 7 Steps To Understand And Balance Chakras, Radiate Energy, And Strengthen Aura"*.

Simply Click the Button Below

OR Go to This Page

http://lifehacksworld.com/free

BONUS #2: More Free & Discounted Books & Products

Do you want to receive more Free/Discounted Books or Products?

We have a mailing list where we send out our new Books or Products when they go free or with a discount on Amazon. Click on the link below to sign up for Free & Discount Book & Product Promotions.

=> Sign Up for Free & Discount Book & Product Promotions <=

OR Go to this URL

http://zbit.ly/1WBb1Ek

Made in the USA
Columbia, SC
18 October 2023